There is (still) love here

There is (still) love here

Dean Atta

Nine
Arches
Press

There is (still) love here
Dean Atta

ISBN: 978-1913437503
eISBN: 978-1913437510

Cover artwork: 'Falling Deeper' © Sanna Räsänen, 2022.

First published September 2022 by:

Nine Arches Press
Unit 14, Sir Frank Whittle Business Centre,
Great Central Way, Rugby.
CV21 3XH
United Kingdom

www.ninearchespress.com

Printed in the United Kingdom by:
Imprint Digital

Nine Arches Press is supported using public funding by Arts Council England.

Supported using public funding by
ARTS COUNCIL
ENGLAND

for Faye

Contents

On Days When

you feel like a wilting garden,
gather yourself, roll up your lawn,
bouquet your flowers,
embrace your weeds.

You are a wild thing playing
at being tame.
You are rich with life beneath
 the surface.

You don't have to show leaf
and petal to be living.
You are soil and insect and root.

How to be a Poet

When your mum loves you unconditionally, say,
Mother, your love is so cliché.

Seek rejection.
Relate to roadkill. Let life crash into you.

Embrace the pain of others when you have none of your own.
Write poems on your phone.

Be at one with technology and at odds with nature.
Be a natural disaster but blame society.

Be a contradiction.
Take your time to rush.
Hurry up and wait.

Do average things but expect to be great.
Look at things differently.
Close your eyes and feel.

Stand out in the sun and pretend to be a flower.
See all people as flowers.
Try and fail to be the sun.

Blame your mum.
Blame your dad.
Blame everything you never had.

Don't rhyme without reason.
Don't hang on to the pencil shavings of life.
Refuse to stay sharp, keep writing.

Five Litres of Blue

I used to think the blood in this body
was five litres of blue,
that only when I bled was it red.

I looked it up and found out
the blue of our veins is a trick of the light.
Human blood is always red,
sometimes crimson, sometimes bright.

Where do blue feelings come from?
I could be at the table with family: blue.
In a nightclub with friends: blue.
In the arms of a lover: blue.

Writing this poem for you: I used to
think of writing as some kind of bleeding.
That colour people stop and notice,
red of accidents, homicide or self-harm.

I used to think the blood in this body
was five litres of blue. How else
could I explain blue feelings to you?

Signet

Your engraved ring reads D.M.P.

if I hadn't changed my surname
this would have been left to me

we are making each other pay
for an inherited debt
your brother   my father

the push and pull between us
an elastic band in the hands of a restless student

we have grown with this tension
yet never snapped back at each other

and without fail
every time you would drive me home
you would call out 'I love you' as I exited the car

I wanted to crush and crumple you – screaming
'I would trade a million uncles for just one father
drive your brother back and make him love me!'

instead I said nothing

not 'I love you too'
not 'I love you too much'

not 'I wish you were my father
so I could have kept my surname'

I turned my key in the front door
I didn't turn back

I heard your engine humming
you hadn't gone

you were waiting.

The Making

after Shailja Patel

Make it from scraps of attention
your father scattered
across your timeline.
The two times he came to see
you on stage.
The one time he visited you
at university.
Gather and add them
to the scrapbook
of love, advice and guidance.
How Uncle D told you
a relationship relies on compromise.
How Uncle T showed you
that even when falling apart
you can still make small
but significant repairs for others.

Make your mother the spine
to this book.
Make it sing kind words.
Make it to find out what words can fix
and what they cannot.
Make it for your mother's approval.
Make it selfishly sometimes.
Make it in secret,
in public, in meditation.
Make it a prayer.
Pray to the earth,

the universe, the light inside yourself.
Make it a mantra.
Make it to forgive   yourself.
Make it to fix what's been broken.
When you break, make no apologies.

Writer in Residence

She says the badge is a barrier. I have to wear the badge
to remind myself I have a job to do.

Outside, I sometimes pretend I'm wearing a friend badge,
uncle badge, son badge, brother badge, I often forget

where I put my nephew badge, grandson badge, and I keep losing
my boyfriend badge. Sometimes I'm wearing two or three at once,

Christmases and funerals my chest is heavy with the weight of them
pinned to my shirt. When alone, I take them all off,

breathe in and out deeply. Poetry is a badge I wear,
as heavy as the rest, something else to get off my chest.

What Do You See?

I don't think
you see a person;
you see a raised fist,
you see a rainbow,
and, if I like you,
you might see a grinning-face emoji.

I see untranslated potential
trapped within the language of thieves.

My slick tongue speaks
coloniser spells,
but if I cut it out I will be mute.

So, if I must, I will speak hashtag,
I will speak meme.

I will be heard, I will be seen.

Stony Eyes of History

Submerged in a river.
Buried. For centuries

I remain undisturbed.
There is light. I am dredged.

Gloved archaeologists,
conservationists, historians

and students in turn
misinterpret, misrepresent,

misremember me.
They hypothesise who

I was when whole,
no idea I can see them

through stony eyes.
Though I have sight,

my sense of self fails
to return to me. I am

barely a body. I stood
for something, once.

Now, an accidental bust.
No arms to defend myself,

no legs to run away,
no genitalia to reproduce.

They take pictures,
make a plaster cast,

lock me in a vault
where I no longer see

who tells my story.

British Citizenship Test

The Guardian ran a sample online,
I got nine out of the ten questions right.
It didn't say which one I'd got wrong
but it was of no consequence to me,
my passport burgundy and well-used.
Border Control is merely a formality,
never afraid of being refused entry,
Britain has always been home to me.

Britain is my mother's cluttered house;
it needs a lick of paint in most places,
it needs cleaning a little more often,
the television stays on a bit too long.
Broken things have a unique charm,
you find a way of getting used to them,
a way to shut the door or turn the tap
that most visitors would find bizarre.

I imagine what the questions would be
if this home had its own citizenship test:
Which Greek word do we use to refer
to the living room? How many months
of the year do we keep the heating on?
I would be impressed if you knew
but more concerned with offering you
a cup of tea, asking if you were hungry.

The Door

I wonder how
my Cypriot grandfather lived
in England for forty-six years without
central heating.

'The door,' he would shout
whenever I stepped
into his living room, not trusting me
to close it.

Cold air trying
to repatriate the room,
one electric heater

our only defence. British-born
but heat-loving,
my home has central heating on
in every room

at least nine months of the year;
mother and I make a mock-
Mediterranean.

My grandfather never paid
to heat his whole house –

it was never really home and he knew
the heat would be waiting
on his return.

No Ascension

You are in hospital, so we buy plane tickets.
You are dying when we reach your bedside.
You are dead, so we wear black for forty days.
Forty days are over but I'm still wearing black.

In London, no one knows why.
In Cyprus, we moved as one
black cloud of grief, the whole family
dressed in the same colour.

Either side of your grave I was Black.
And this isn't a eulogy, it's about me.
How I haven't cleaned the mud from your grave
off the shoes I bought for your funeral.

How often I look at the photos I took of you
smiling, dying, dead, and being buried.
How your watch and prayer beads are in the draw
of this desk I am writing this poem on.

How grief makes much more sense to me
than feeling depressed when times are good.
How a grandfather is meant to die old
and surrounded by his family, just as you did.

How my notebook is a grave and my laptop
is a grave, how my phone is a grave and my bed
is a grave, and there was no ascension after
forty days. And I have stayed buried, with you.

Preparing for the Worst

I ask my friend how she coped
with her mother's death.

'I'm afraid I wouldn't be able
to cope, if mine were to die.'

She reaches across the table,
her hand lands on my forearm.

'Is she sick?' She asks, with watery eyes.

'No,' I reply.

Her hand lifts
like one half of a drawbridge.

She leans back, looks away.

I know instantly
I have broken an unspoken rule

of talking about my mother
as anything other than immortal.

Fragments of Faye

I've already forgotten
the weight of the coffin.
If it was heavy
because I was the weakest
or light
because the other five
being taller
carried most of it.

I know you
were not in there
just like my grandfather wasn't
the body
we were allowed
to escort
to the mortuary.

I cannot believe
I carried you
on my shoulder.
Before I left the hospital
each time
I held your hand
I kissed your forehead
I said goodbye.

*

In your kitchen, I prepare
the vegetables for the juicer.

I tell you I'm upset
you refused medical treatment
when it was offered
but I respect your decision.
I don't think a juice cleanse
is enough to beat cancer,
but it can't hurt, I suppose.

I press the juice, and discard
all the pulp. 'What a waste.'

*

The hospital cinema
is playing *Battle of the Sexes*.

I pretend I haven't seen it.

As they roll your bed
and all its attached equipment
down the corridor, you let me
hold the invitation,
which you call *our tickets*.

'This is my nephew,' you beam
at one of the staff steering your bed.

'I know,' he smiles at me,
'She talks about you all the time.'

*

The second week in
hospital, you are so weak.
They wash you in your bed
but you beg to have a shower
and they agree to use a hoist;
you tell me about it with such glee.
I try to remember you
before your face was gaunt
and your legs were swollen,
before your stomach was a balloon,
before the cancer in your womb
spread. And I remember:

you have come to visit
us at university in Brighton,
you stay with Tracey
and the girls. I come by
in the morning, ready for our day.
They tell me you're still
in the shower. You come down
singing to yourself,
smiling, 'Sorry,' you say,
with a not-sorry shrug,
'I just love a long shower.'

You smile so wide, your
cheekbones so high, your
skin slick with shea butter,
your long locs so neat,
tightly twisted at the roots,
and now you are ready.

Lost in Translation

1. Code Switching

When the last of my friends have left, you say, 'I don't know who you are.' You are preparing a Pot Noodle. I twice offered you a plate of jerk chicken, rice and peas. 'What do you mean?' I ask you, my white university flatmate from Cornwall. I gather emptied plates. Though Brighton is home to us now, I hope I did Jamaica proud, making this dish for mouths more accustomed to recipes from Ghana, Nigeria, Senegal and Uganda. You scratch your headtop between blonde dreadlocks and say, 'You speak one way with your Black friends, another with your gay friends, another with your mum, and differently with me.' 'So what?' I hiss, heart pounding, breath short. Why am I so angry? Why are you crying?

2. 'Who can't hear, must feel'

This warning follows a previous
warning, that you are behaving
in a dangerous, destructive
or displeasing manner.

What you will feel may be immediate,
such as a slap or spanking
from a parent or other elder,
or a consequence down the line,
such as a heartbreak, job loss,
another loss or tragedy.

The person delivering this warning
may also deliver the consequence
or may have the foresight
and wisdom that you lack.

3. Concert Hall

Maybe music doesn't move you the way
it does me. Maybe you're here to judge
but I'm here to enjoy. I relate to the violin
and the bow. I wish to be the conductor.
You are the sheet music, the composer,
the conservatoire. These tickets were gifted
to me and I've come here for a good time.
I've brought my whole self, my history, my body,
the spirit of my ancestors. If I feel the beat,
I will tap my feet, my head and shoulders
will respond to the rise and fall; the tempo.
I hold my breath at a rest. But you look
identical to that symbol of silence, sitting
in your chair. My body freestyles, improvises,
is not of note.

4. UK Black Pride

Bring your own,
rum and coke
or rum and ginger,
a dash of lime,
in a plastic bottle
because security
confiscates glass.
Resent police presence.
Try to believe they are
here to protect you.
Acknowledge elders
seated up on the hill
on picnic blankets
looking over the pulsing
mass of bodies.
Go down and join the mass,
gun fingers and finger snaps.
Feel the joy of being
your whole self.
Take selfies with friends,
ask permission
to take pictures
of pretty strangers
whose genders
you cannot be sure of,
whose beauty
is undeniable,
whose presence
is a blessing,

whose freedom
gives you courage.
Feel a hunger.
Look for the food stall with the longest queue
because you know
what they've got
will be the best.
What you'll get here
is more than
sustenance.
Yes, you will miss
some time dancing –
but full belly,
happy heart.

Pulse

1. Hazardous Material

As we reach the mutual climax
of our love making
they burst in wearing hazmat suits
and set fire to the bed sheets

We run naked and barefoot into the streets
a crowd gathers behind us
coming out of their glass houses
to throw stones

We keep running, hand in hand
a white-knuckle grip, one pulling the other
when he buckles or stops to examine
a fresh cut to the sole of his foot

We run for a year, without looking back
we do not sleep, eat or drink
and, despite our nakedness
we do not think of making love

We will never know what
kept us alive that year
some miracle we suppose
like the one that happens next

We both begin to glow
our veins sing like a chorus of angels
'Hallelujah, we are clean!
Hallelujah, we are clean!'

Our wounds healing before our eyes
we give our miracle blood
as an offering, as thanks to a society
that forced us to see the light.

2. *Tweets after Orlando*

Calum McSwiggan:
'You tell us that you don't mind what we do
as long as we do it behind closed doors
and then you kick down those closed doors
and open fire'

Jeramey Kraatz:
'If you can't wrap your head around
a bar or club as a sanctuary
you've probably never been afraid
to hold someone's hand in public'

Jack O'Brien:
'Waiting time for a gay man
to donate blood: 1 year of no sexual contact
waiting time for a psychopath
to purchase an assault rifle: 3 days'

3. Sanctuary

Banning blood donation from gay men
goes hand-in-hand with the thinking
that would lead someone to massacre us.

When only those who hate us want our blood
and we live in fear of expressing our love
and our sanctuaries don't feel safe anymore.

We must march in the street, meet in public places
perform on stages, raise our voices louder still.
It takes more than a gun to make someone kill.

Stuck in the Mud

These are The Rules:

One person is 'it'
and we run away from them
because they have the power
and the rest of us don't.

If they touch anyone,
that person becomes
stuck, so they can't
move their feet and have to stand
still with their arms out like this, like the letter T,
like Jesus on the cross.

Anyone who is free
can run under their arm,
either arm, it doesn't matter which one,
and they will be made
free again.

*

His touch taught me
a different game

He made The Rules up
        as we played

He was 'it' all the time
I was of a martyr's mind

My idea of winning   trying
to make him happy

but I was slowly   slipping
back into the mud in which

He found me.

        *

Finally, He asks me:

What if
neither of us are 'it'
and we don't stay still long enough
to become stuck?

What if
we roll in the mud
and ditch all The Rules?

Two Black Boys in Paradise

They won't be here forever,
maybe just as long as this poem.
These two Black boys in paradise.
Two Black boys: can you see them?

These two Black boys are free.
These two Black boys are happy.
Black boys are real boys.
Black boys are not just little men.

Do you believe Black boys
are real, like for real for real?
Real Black boys feel.
These two Black boys are a healing.

Did you poison the apple already?
Did you dig up the tree?
Are you trying to plant
these Black boys in the ground?

Did you call them apple thieves?
Did you call the police?
There are no police in paradise.
There are no white people in this paradise.

The two boys in this poem have Black boy names.
They have grown up now,
but their names still suit them.
Masculinity has not been required of them.

They are in love with each other,
and they are in love with themselves.
One kisses the other's Adam's apple.
They don't make babies.

Maybe paradise is just meant for two people at a time.
Maybe it will be two Black girls in paradise next time.
Maybe they won't have to be
boys or girls.

Maybe it will be you in paradise
with that person
you have in mind
right now.

What I Didn't Know Before

after Ada Limón

Our love will die
if it is not watered

with compliments
and gratitude.

How to change
gears on a bike

to make it easier
to go uphill.

To be gentle
squeezing the brakes

going downhill.
How to discover

water in the mountains –
an ear to the ground

following its flow.
The difference

between a coot
and a moorhen.

You teach me
to recognise

that white shield
on a coots' head.

I teach my niece.
Now, when she says,

'Look, a coot!'
She points to name

our love,
gliding on the water.

Circassian Circle

A therapist tiptoes towards
        a question about my relationship:

                'Who takes the female role?'

'We're two men,' my head tilts.

                Her eyes dart around the room
                before they settle on the carpet
                between us, kitten-heeled feet
                shuffle as she shifts in her seat.

I wonder if she's trying to ask:
Who's top and who's bottom?
My man and I aren't opposites.
I check, 'What's the female role?'

                She side-steps the question
                and changes the subject,
                leaving it to spiral in my mind.

I think of partner dancing:
how someone must lead
and someone must follow
but how it needn't be gendered.

I think of how our neighbour
calls us 'lads' and so we are.
How restaurant staff call us
'gentlemen' and so we are.

My partner wears nail varnish
on weekends but removes it
from his fingernails for work:
keeping only toenails painted –
his personal act of rebellion.

I wear makeup, a costume
and high heels on stage.
I'm applauded. I'm reminded
I'm beautiful and brave
but take a taxi home to be safe.

> I don't see that therapist
> anymore but her question
> keeps wrong-footing me.

Finally, I land on an answer:

If he knows the steps, I follow.
When I'm confident, I lead.
When neither of us know,
we look around to realise,
this isn't just a partner dance,
we're part of a queer ceilidh
with so many hands to hold,
some painted nails, some plain,
no pair exactly the same.

Category Is Books

How long will we be socially distancing?
I think of my family in London, Cyprus,
and Switzerland, how on 8th August 2019
we were crammed into Gay's the Word

for my book launch and farewell party,
how you and I left for our new home
the next day, how we found Category Is
Books and a new community waiting,

how we're building a life together brick
by brick south of the River Clyde but
so far north of our previous London homes.
Your job means you're here for four years

but I feel like I could leave at any time,
how I only brought the essential items,
like clothes and important documents
and only a small selection of my books.

The rest are with my mother in London
who is working her way through them
alone during lockdown. Here in Glasgow,
this shelf-space, a lack of commitment.

Yours and Mine

You keep bringing home plants.
At first, I say it's your responsibility
to water them but I cannot help
but notice when their soil is drying.

When we're both home,
glasses of water and mugs of tea
are the way we check in and show
each other how much we care.

Millilitre by millilitre, we flood
each other with love. Our two mugs,
a gift from Sonia, say 'Yours' and
'Mine' but we haven't decided

which is yours and which is mine.
Is everything ours? You put more
plants on the empty bookshelves
and they look so at home.

You're painting the walls in our
bedroom this week, litres of
Cape Verde on once white walls.
You want it cosy and den-like.

I think of a den like going to bed
with no expectation of sleep,
dreaming with eyes wide open.
A den is an endeavour made

of borrowed materials, temporary
and precarious but so much
more than the sum of its parts.
Our life together feels den-like.

Last night we slept on the futon
in our guest room; we play
at being visitors to our own life.
Today you decorate and I write.

As I write this last line, I can smell
Cape Verde paint drying.

Letter to London

I wish you would find a way
to say you miss me,
not through my mother
or my friends. I wish the bells
of St Paul's Cathedral
would call my name. I wish
Shakespeare's Globe
would creak for me
to walk its boards again.
I wish paint would weep
from every canvas in Tate Modern
and Tate Britain
and fill the Thames
with a rainbow in my honour.
I wish your pigeons
would fly to Glasgow, lift me up
and carry me home.

Strawberry Thief

William Morris curtains
surround the dining table
nested in the bay window.
These thrushes never able
to reach the strawberries.

Maybe they're waiting
for someone to wish them
bon appétit, as we do
with each other. Neither of us
French, but we don't say
the equivalent in Greek,
Jamaican patois or Italian.

We're two Englishmen
in Scotland. Tonight we eat
Shepherd's Pie. You've made it
for me for the first time.
It's my comfort food,
reminds me of home-home,

my mother's home
in London, where we call
the living room the 'sala'
even though the Greek is 'salóni' –
village Greek, she tells me.

She is alone in her sala.
Her daughter and granddaughters
nearby, but unable to visit.

Me, here, in Glasgow.
The rest of her family
in Cyprus and Switzerland.

You don't miss your family,
you admit to me.
Your Shepherd's Pie
is better than my mother's,
I admit to you.

On Giving

after Kahlil Gibran

Let's pretend

        we asked for rain,
        so we can marvel at the generosity of the sky.

Let's pretend

        we asked for all this time
        alone together, just you and I,
        so we could grow like houseplants,
        observed only by each other.

Let's pretend

        the postman is a friend, just popping by.
        When he looks me in the eye, I say, 'Thanks, pal.'
        Then, I have an envelope and a box in either hand
        and postman-friend is gone.

Let's pretend

        the postman is my niece
        bringing me gifts of a leaf and a stone.
        I hold both hands out at equal height.
        They place the leaf on my left palm
        and the stone on my right.
        I tilt like scales to demonstrate
        their difference in weight.
        Postman-niece lets out a small giggle
        before they are gone, again.

Four Plantains in a One-Pound Bowl

Walking home from the Post Office
on Victoria Road, you call out to me.

Holding you, I feel closer to myself.
You feel like a bargain, but it's been

so long since I've bought plantain,
I cannot remember how much you

should be. Twenty-five pence each
seems a steal. Paying for a one-pound

purchase by contactless payment
feels naughty. No questions asked.

I intend to fry you, to accompany
yesterday's leftovers, jerk chicken

with rice and peas, but as I slice,
the knife glides so smoothly through

you, that I am curious how ripe,
how soft and sweet it would be to

eat you raw. I place a slice of you
in my mouth, and you taste just like

your smaller cousin: the banana.
I know cooking will only enhance

your flavour, but I am so tempted
to devour you exactly as you are.

How to Make Louvi

Serving suggestion: read aloud with a partner

Weigh 400g of black-eyed beans
soak in a bowl of cold water overnight
in the morning, check
to see if they're ready to be boiled

realise 400g expands
to a monumental amount
too much for just you and your partner

drain the beans
transfer to a stock pot
add boiling water
simmer on a low heat
salt the water
add two bay leaves
leave for 45 minutes to an hour
check intermittently

if you feel nervous
the pot might boil over
or the water might
evaporate completely
or the beans might go mushy
these are irrational fears
but it's okay to have irrational fears
you've never done it this way
you usually use tinned beans
you couldn't find any
in your local shops
your partner swears
there weren't any
in the supermarket

when the beans feel almost
soft enough to eat
steam spinach in a colander over your pot
for a further 5 minutes

sigh
a long sigh
as the spinach wilts

turn off the hob
spoon your desired portions
of beans and spinach into two bowls

miss your family

into each bowl, squeeze
the juice of half a lemon

admire the weeping sun
in your hand

add a few glugs of olive oil
for added crunch, chop
and sprinkle on spring onion
and

finally

a pinch of salt.

Translate This Sentence

'Η οικογένεια μου είναι
πολύ μακριά από εδώ.'

'My family are
very far away from here.'

Another correct solution:
'My family is
very far away from here.'

Whether 'is' or 'are',
my family are far,

and learning Greek
does not bring them
closer to me right now.

I cannot comprehend
this situation but I can focus
my attention εδώ. Here.

Στο τραπέζι με την αγάπη μου
(At the table with my love)

The world offers itself
to him and he thinks:
I must have it all.

The Greek word for table
pronounced trapézi
half-sounds like a trap.

I ask him to sit
for a meal with me,
serve him my love.

The Greek word for love
is pronounced agápi
but he is agape –

adjective (of a person's mouth)
wide open in surprise,
wonder –

he cannot believe
that I love him,
that love is enough.

Empathy

You do not have to be a flower
in a vase to see the tragedy of it.

As a gesture, I understand why
he brings them home each week.

But groceries tell me he loves me
more than this beautiful death bouquet.

Each morning another one drooping,
drained of colour, dropping

petals. They look like they're gasping,
no roots, no chance of lasting.

Broken Bench

Out back behind
our blue recycling bins
still sittable despite
one missing slat.
I am here looking
onto this small
patch of green watching
neighbours' clothes
and sheets swaying.

We're not allowed
to sit on benches
in the park, so this
is my only chance
to sit in the sun.
In the park you must
run, walk, or cycle
you must keep moving
you cannot be still.

No Headspace

I am suspended
on the exhale

I want to stay here
in the moment

before the inhale
when anxiety returns

with the news
and my Twitter feed

and my family
on WhatsApp

maybe I shouldn't
meditate using my phone

I am suspended
between heartbeats

between solitude
and anticipation

a tinnitus fear
always in my ear

unable to mute
or make peace.

Nightshift

You taste of toothpaste
and I taste of coffee.

I'm ready for the day
and you're ready for bed.

You're an essential
worker and I'm a writer.

I've felt many things
but never essential.

Beachcombing at Night

I find a broken compass
behind his right ear,
two Euros behind his left,
bent spoons in each armpit,
AA batteries behind both
of his knees. He hands me
a torch, nothing happens
when I flick the switch.

Ah! I swap the batteries
for the ones from his knees,
but they only make this dim,
flickering light.

Sensing Something is Wrong

My boyfriend's kisses
taste like cheese and marmite.

He smells like the cocoa butter
that stops his sterilised hands
getting too dry.

He sounds like Stephen Fry
when he tells me random facts
about etymology.

My boyfriend speaks English,
Italian, French, Spanish
and um pouco de portugues.

He looks like he could be
from any of these countries,
his olive skin, his dark hair
and large nose.

My boyfriend looks like his father
when he's angry and knowing this
means I'm now part of his family.

He feels so far away sometimes,
like when a patient has died.
But he doesn't want to talk about it.

A Letter to the Man in the Next Room

It's not that I'm sick
of your face
or tired of your voice.
I just know them so well,
I can predict
your facial expressions,
playful blowing of a kiss,
gentle stroke of my foot
when we span the sofa together,
my legs on your lap.

I want you
to ask a question
I've never been asked before,
put a sentence together
I've never heard before.
I don't want you to be a poet,
I know enough of those, but
I know you have many words
locked inside.

Tenement

I don't know if I want to be here
in our two bedroom tenement flat in Battlefield
or in the listed building on Queen's Park Drive
you take me to view.

'If it's warmth you're after, a tenement might not
be for you,' says one half of the gay couple
showing us around their home of six years,
as if I don't know the cold of tenement living.

'We've decided it's time to upgrade
to a house,' the other half tells us, as if looking down
the property and relationship ladder.
After the viewing, we slip into a two-day argument.

Then, it's Sunday: we clean as we do each week,
radio playing, no need to speak. I wonder
how to clean the radiator gaps, grimacing teeth of heat,
gathering dust for the two years we've lived here.

I purchase a cleaning tool that boasts
removing dust will reduce the risk of fire.
I'd never thought of dust, fragments of us
and our living, at risk of catching alight.

I'll wait, again, for Sunday
to dislodge dust, doubt and fear,
along with cruel words we've spoken here
accumulating in hard-to-reach places.

Mundane Magic

This is our new normal / we go into the garden
fortnightly to cut my hair

the extension cable fed through / our bedroom window
clippers plugged in

I sit shirtless / on the fold-out metal chair
as the clippers buzz

we begin to float / you me and the chair
eight legs in the air

the extension cable / anchors us to our home
as the haircut continues

tiny particles of me / carried off in the wind
this mundane magic

all I have to do is sit here / we've been doing this
for the best part of a year.

When

we take a break
from arguing
to make two cups of tea

when we are running
but too far apart to talk
there is still love here

when we listen to the radio
I know I could leave you
as easily as changing the station

when we are hiking
and I am struggling
and you seem impatient

when I stop for water
the wind whistles in my ear
there is still love here.

I Never Asked for Another City

Arriving back in London,
I think: *Why have we done this?*

I don't want The Shard
or the Docklands Light Railway.

I don't want Fenchurch Street
or the peopled walk to Tower Hill.

I don't want the Tower of London.
I don't know which part of the world I want

or which part of the world wants me
but I know I don't want it all to myself.

I see a canopy of trees, a forest floor,
a body of water, a shelter.

If you cannot be my shelter,
could you be a tree, shelter me incidentally?

Dear Brokenhearted Man

I am you and I am healing.
I'm writing to you because

I want you to know
it's going to be okay.

You're going to Faye's funeral today
and afterwards

you're booked to perform poems
at a medical school.

You feel guilty
because you opted out

of writing a poem for the funeral.
You'll read a poem chosen by Faye's family.

It's okay.
You will write about Faye one day.   Go

to your show tonight.
You'll notice his nose at first

and then his eyes.
He'll give your grief a smile.

You'll have sex with this stranger.
You won't tell him about Faye right away

but he knows
enough about life and death

and he knows
how to restart a heart.

Murmuration (Faye as a Flock of Starlings)

Boy of grief and gravity
    you marvel at my majesty
        and imagine being one of me
            one of many, one of many
                to some you are predator
                    to others you are prey
                just like me, a Black body
            in motion, following
        tilting, turning on a wing
    one of many, one of many
but no less than any other
    no need to run for cover
        when you are shoulder-
            to-shoulder with siblings
                blood is not the only song
                    to make a family from
                you will learn instinctually
            a spontaneous choreography
    necessary for your survival.

Acknowledgements and Thanks

To my family, my friends and my partner: It would be impossible for me to fit all of your beauty and brilliance into any number of poems. I'm so grateful for each and every moment I spend with you. The few moments I write about aren't any more important than those that pass without remark.

To my agent Becky Thomas and editor Jane Commane: Thank you for helping me realise this book.

To Sanna Räsänen: Thank you so much for your stunning cover art. It was love at first sight when I saw that gorgeous image!

To Andrew McMillan, Malika Booker, Pascale Petit and Salena Godden: Thank you for your incredibly kind endorsements for this book. You have been guiding lights in the poetry community for me and so many.

I feel such immense gratitude to my mentors, Benjamin Zephaniah, Charlie Dark and Peter Kahn, and every facilitator of every workshop I've ever attended, especially Hannah Lavery for leading the very necessary and nurturing Writers of Colour Writing Group over the past few years. Much love to the OGs: Jacob Sam-La Rose, Joseph Coelho and Steven Camden aka Polarbear.

I will be forever indebted to the Kiln Theatre, Lyric Hammersmith, Riverside Studios and Roundhouse Studios for providing safe and nurturing environments for me to find community, contextualise my voice and develop my craft. The connections made in your buildings led me to discover Arvon, First Story, Keats House Poets' Forum, Malika's Poetry Kitchen, New Writing South, Mouthy Poets, Open Book, Scottish BPOC Writers Network, Spoken Word Educators, Spread the Word and Writing Our Legacy. These organisations and programmes have been integral to my professional development and I feel so humbled and grateful to reflect on this. Not forgetting the spoken word poetry community across the U.K. and the world that has provided platforms for me to connect directly with audiences.

I felt positively giddy compiling a list of where poems in this book have been previously published: *100 Queer Poems* (Vintage, 2022) *ANTHROPOCENE, bath magg, Butcher's Dog, Dazed & Confused, Field Notes on Survival* (Bad Betty Press, 2020), *Finished Creatures, Glass Poetry, Gutter, harana poetry, Ink Sweat & Tears, Metaphors for a Black Future Zine, More Fiya* (Canongate, 2022), *Re•creation: A Queer Poetry Anthology* (Stewed Rhubarb Press, 2022), *Second Place Rosette: Poems about Britain* (The Emma Press, 2018), *STRIKE!, The Dizziness of Freedom* (Bad Betty Press, 2018), *The Frogmore Papers, The Selkie, The Stockholm Review of Literature* and *Where We Find Ourselves: Poems and Stories of Maps and Mapping from UK writers of the global majority* (Arachne Press, 2021). Thank you to the editors of these and every publication that has ever published my poetry!

'British Citizenship Test' was commissioned by *Dazed & Confused*. 'Category Is Books', 'Two Black Boys in Paradise' and 'Yours and Mine' were commissioned by The Courtauld Research Forum. 'Circassian Circle' was commissioned by the National Theatre of Scotland. 'Stony Eyes of History' was commissioned by Keats House Museum. I am so thankful for these commissions and how they asked me questions I hadn't yet asked.